TRAVELING SAVANNAH * A GIRL'S GUIDE
OFF THE MAP FAVORITES OF A LOCAL GIRL

ISBN-13: 978-0-6153445-6-0

ISBN-10: 0-6153445-6-9

Printed in Canada by Transcontinental Printing

DEDICATION

This book is dedicated to my most favorite girlfriend and eternal best friend, my mom, Shelley Shultz. Mom, you have taught me the importance of girlfriends and doing the things you love with people who make you happy. This book is for you and for the other mothers and daughters out there who know how powerful and unique the mother-daughter bond is and how important it is to embrace it.

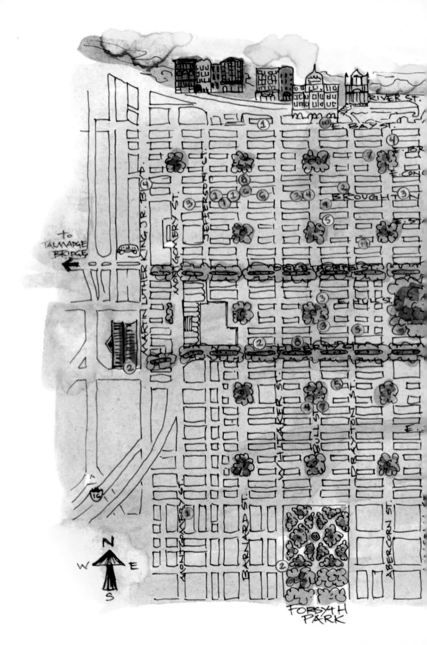

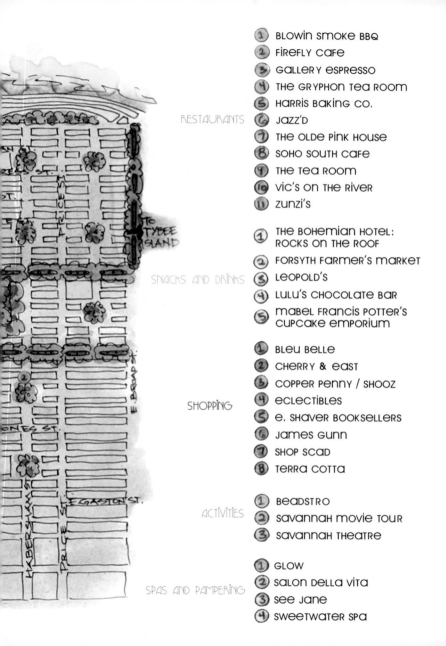

RESTAURANTS

1. BLOWIN SMOKE BBQ
2. FIREFLY CAFE
3. GALLERY ESPRESSO
4. THE GRYPHON TEA ROOM
5. HARRIS BAKING CO.
6. JAZZ'D
7. THE OLDE PINK HOUSE
8. SOHO SOUTH CAFE
9. THE TEA ROOM
10. VIC'S ON THE RIVER
11. ZUNZI'S

SNACKS AND DRINKS

1. THE BOHEMIAN HOTEL: ROCKS ON THE ROOF
2. FORSYTH FARMER'S MARKET
3. LEOPOLD'S
4. LULU'S CHOCOLATE BAR
5. MABEL FRANCIS POTTER'S CUPCAKE EMPORIUM

SHOPPING

1. BLEU BELLE
2. CHERRY & EAST
3. COPPER PENNY / SHOOZ
4. ECLECTIBLES
5. E. SHAVER BOOKSELLERS
6. JAMES GUNN
7. SHOP SCAD
8. TERRA COTTA

ACTIVITIES

1. BEADSTRO
2. SAVANNAH MOVIE TOUR
3. SAVANNAH THEATRE

SPAS AND PAMPERING

1. GLOW
2. SALON DELLA VITA
3. SEE JANE
4. SWEETWATER SPA

INTRO

I am one of the lucky girls who grew up in Savannah and am now living here as an adult. A lawyer by day, I love making jewelry, scrapbooking, and spending time with my husband and four dogs (yes, you read that correctly - we each had two before we met, so voila…instant family!) I love Savannah, and as an avid shopper (don't tell my husband), eater (I tried dieting for 6 months before my wedding and was quite cranky, so now I choose to embrace my chubbiness), and do-er, I have some favorite places around town that I wanted to share with you. I realized that while there are a myriad of generic Savannah travel books with cool sites and restaurants, there are none specifically geared toward women. Many of the places in this book are off the beaten path, and I would recommend contacting them prior to going, as, unfortunately, shops and restaurants can come and go, no matter how fabulous I think they are. While I consulted all of these venues before using their names, I did not allow any restaurants or shops to "purchase a spot" in the book. These are my personal favorite places, and I think you will love them, too! Enjoy Savannah, girls!

Meredith

KEY

 Reservations recommended

 Not recommended for men (unless they are gay or very comfortable with their sexuality)

 Pets welcome

 Kinda pricey

TABLE OF CONTENTS

activities

spas and pampering

where to meet men

when to come to savannah

sample days

books to read to get psyched for your savannah trip

RESTAURANTS

BeLLa's itaLian café

4420 HaBersHam street
912-354-4005
monDay-friDay 11:30-2
monDay-tHursDay 5-9
friDay-saturDay 5-10
sunDay 5-8
www.BeLLascafe.com

Bella's has been the go-to Italian place in Savannah for as long as I can remember. While not strictly a ladies' place, I have spent enough evenings here drinking a glass of wine with my ladies over a bowl of pasta to consider it a fabulous girls spot. I haven't had a single meal there that I didn't love, but they can go a little heavy on the sauce, so if you don't like a lot of sauce, ask for a little or get it on the side. All entrees come with their house salad which I can only describe as a slice of heaven. I have no idea what they put in their dressing, and I cannot replicate it for the life of me, but it's awesome. Combined with the breadsticks with marinara and garlic butter…bellisimo! (I think that's Italian for something good.)

BLOWIN' SMOKE
514 MARTIN LUTHER KING, JR. BOULEVARD
912-231-2385
SUNDAY-THURSDAY 11-9
FRIDAY-SATURDAY 11-10
WWW.BLOWINSMOKEBBQ.COM

Another one that is not strictly for girls but happens to be one of my faves is Blowin' Smoke barbecue. It is out of the main downtown area, for sure, but Brian, the owner, has created the cutest little nook over off Martin Luther King Blvd. There is an outdoor patio (and tent in the wintertime), and they often have live music. There is always a corn-hole game (it's that game where you throw little bean bags into a board with holes in it – I never knew that was the official name until recently) going on the patio, too. Great way to burn off those fried pickles, a must-have barbeque side dish. My hubby and I threw a couples' baby shower there for some friends of ours and called it a baby-Q. I thought it was quite the clever name, but some people said it sounded like we'd be roasting babies on a spit. I find those people to be truly disturbed.

BONA BELLA YACHT CLUB

2740 Livingston Avenue
912-352-3133
Monday, Wednesday, Thursday & Friday 5-10
Closed Tuesdays
Saturday- Sunday 12-10
www.bonabellayachtclub.com

If you are looking for a cool spot to have drinks and dinner on the water, you will not find it downtown. You have to venture about 15 minutes from downtown to Bona Bella Yacht Club. It's not really a yacht club anymore, but many patrons still come by boat, because the restaurant is situated on a deck overlooking the water with a large dock below. As a boat is still on our many-years-down-the-road wish list, I will sometimes ride to Bona Bella with my car windows open and then walk down onto the dock before seeing the hostess just to give myself the windblown, fresh-off-the-boat look. The restaurant is often reserved for events, so you will definitely want to call first before trekking out there. It is so worth it, though, once you get there. There is something about the smell of the salt marsh and the sound of the water that just screams Savannah. Can't you just taste the margaritas?

19.....RESTAURANTS

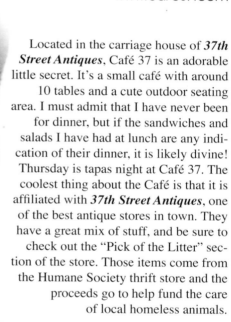

café 37

205 e. 37TH STReeT
912-236-8533
TUeSDay-SaTURDay 11-3
SUNDay 10-3
THURSDay-SaTURDay 6-9
www.cafe37.com

Located in the carriage house of *37th Street Antiques*, Café 37 is an adorable little secret. It's a small café with around 10 tables and a cute outdoor seating area. I must admit that I have never been for dinner, but if the sandwiches and salads I have had at lunch are any indication of their dinner, it is likely divine! Thursday is tapas night at Café 37. The coolest thing about the Café is that it is affiliated with *37th Street Antiques*, one of the best antique stores in town. They have a great mix of stuff, and be sure to check out the "Pick of the Litter" section of the store. Those items come from the Humane Society thrift store and the proceeds go to help fund the care of local homeless animals.

FIREFLY CAFÉ

321 HABERSHAM STREET
912-234-1971
MONDAY-THURSDAY 10:30-9
FRIDAY 10:30-9:30
SATURDAY 9-9:30
SUNDAY 9-3
WWW.FIREFLYCAFEGA.COM

On a cute corner off Troup Square is Firefly, a home to many memories for me and one of my besties, Rachel. We worked at this adorable café when it was known as 321 Café (due to its address of 321 Habersham Street) when we were teenagers. We often got scolded for dancing when a song came on the sound system that required our complete attention (i.e., Belinda Carlisle– Heaven is a Place on Earth) or putting embarrassing things about each other on the daily specials board. It was, and still is, a great place for breakfast, lunch, and dinner. Although, you might want to keep an eye out for the woman who orders a full meal for her imaginary friend. It inevitably gets boxed up by the servers who know her by name. And yes, my friends, they now serve alcohol. There was an issue with their alcohol license when Rachel and I worked there, but looking back that was probably a good thing for us high school girls.

GALLERY ESPRESSO

234 BULL STREET
912-233-5348
MONDAY-FRIDAY 7:30-10
SATURDAY-SUNDAY 8-11
WWW.GALLERYESPRESSO.COM

On the corner of Chippewa Square is a quaint little café and coffee house called Gallery Espresso. At first glance, one might think it's just a coffee shop, but how wrong you would be. Inside you will find fabulous little gifty knick-knacks, a rather impressive lunch menu, some amazing desserts, and a rotating showcase of local artwork. Usually they have pretty good background music, too – not too loud and not too elevator. Any place that plays Madonna and Tiffany during the same cup of coffee is a friend of mine. I spent a few weeks studying for the bar exam there but eventually had to relocate when I realized that sitting at a table was not burning off the delicious baked goods I was eating daily while studying. While it's true that the brain needs fat to function, it's also true that the pants need to button in order to not look ridiculous. Before leaving, check out **Savannah Art Works** just a couple of doors down on Bull Street. It's full of artsy knick-knacks. My husband and I are on the rather short side of the height spectrum, and we could never reach the fan and light pulls in our house without jumping or standing on furniture. We found these beautiful fan pulls at **Savannah Art Works** that changed our lives immensely. Even though my jumping skills have suffered, we now look far less stupid turning our lights and fans on and off.

THE GRYPHON TEA ROOM

337 BULL STREET
912-525-5880
MONDAY-SATURDAY 10-6

Believe it or not, this was an old
pharmacy. When you walk in,
you will totally see it. It's a gorgeous building – be sure to check
out the detail of the ceiling and
counters. The restaurant has been
re-done with a bit of a SCAD
(Savannah College of Art and
Design) flair, with some bright
colors and funkiness. The food is
great, too! They have something
on their menu that I find absolutely brilliant, and I wish more
restaurants would do it: for the
indecisive women who want to
try more than one salad, you can
pick three and get little portions
of each one! Total rocket science
for the palate!

HɑRRiS BɑKiNG COMPɑNY
102 e. LiBeRTY STReeT # 101
912-233-6400
MONDɑY-SUNDɑY 7:30—5:30
WWW.HɑRRiSBɑKiNGCO.com

If you are moseying around downtown and are looking for a place to grab a bite for breakfast or lunch, this is your place. Conveniently located on Drayton Street near the corner of Liberty (and yes, I do realize that their actual address is on Liberty Street, but I find that to be somewhat misleading), they have fresh sandwiches, salads, pastries. My favorite is their turkey bacon Panini with a side salad. Their house salad is tossed in this ranch dressing (who doesn't love ranch!?) and is super delish. They also have flavored syrups that you can add to your tea. As lame as it sounds, this totally made my day on an especially stressful workday when I walked to Harris Baking for lunch. Who'd have thought some peach syrup (that wasn't even Schnapps!) could have that much of a positive impact on one's day?

JAZZ'D

52 BARNARD STREET (BEHIND THE GAP)
912-236-7777
SUNDAY-SATURDAY 4 - UNTIL
(LIVE MUSIC TUESDAY-SUNDAY)
WWW.JAZZDSAVANNAH.COM

This is one of my favorite places to come on a girls' night for dinner. It's tapas-style dining, so everyone can share and you don't look like a pig ordering a few dishes. They also have some of the most incredible martini flavors (second only to **Lulu's Chocolate Bar** (Page 57) and live jazz music most nights. The only downfall about Jazz'd is that on the live music nights, it can get a little noisy as the night goes on… but let's be honest, after a few martinis, we don't make any sense anyway, and it's probably just as well that no one can hear us.

The Olde Brick House

RESTAURANT & TAVERN

THE OLDE PINK HOUSE

23 ABERCORN STREET
912-232-4286
TUESDAY-THURSDAY 11-10:30
FRIDAY-SATURDAY 11-11
SUNDAY-MONDAY 5-10:30

Now, this one you might spot in a typical travel book, but with a name like "The Olde Pink House," how can it not be perfect for women? There is a piano bar down below and a bar area with some outside tables (weather permitting) on the Saint Julian Street side of the house and a couple of levels of inside dining. The downstairs bar with the fireplace is ideal for cooler months. They recently opened for lunch, and while it's a little on the pricey side, it's worth the splurge. For dinner, it is quaint and Southern, and not the pretentious kind of Southern – just classy. My hubby and I went there for an anniversary dinner, and it was just divine. Their menu boasts of seafood, pasta, steak, and others, all done with unique combinations of sauces and sides. They have a fantastic seafood bisque in the cooler months, and my husband thinks their fish tacos are a far better lunch than any leftovers I would pack for us. He's right.

SOHO SOUTH CAFÉ

12 W. LIBERTY ST.
912-233-1633
SUNDAY BRUNCH 11-4
MONDAY-SATURDAY 11-4
WWW.SOHOSOUTHCAFE.COM

Soho just might be my all-time favorite place to lunch in Savannah. In fact, I love it so much that this is where my bridal shower was. Probably the two coolest things about Soho are the fact that it is a converted old garage and that it doubles as an art gallery for local artists. Some of the artwork is big and pricey – like large canvases costing hundreds of dollars or more – but some pieces are smaller and more affordable (i.e., paintings for $75-150 and hand-painted note cards for $15-30). So, order your lunch – great sandwiches, salads, quiches, etc. - and then walk around and shop. Try to get there before 11:45, because there is a mad rush of a lunch crowd that comes right around noon, and after that, there can be a bit of a wait. There is a great menu – mostly sandwiches and salads, but I have not gone with anyone who did not love their meal (including my hubby whom I had to drag there, and he finally admitted they in fact have one of the best burgers in town! Who knew?) Make sure you at least get a cup of the tomato basil bisque – it's to die for! It used to be a special, but it was so popular, it's now a permanent fixture on the menu. Great for Sunday brunch, too, but get there early if you don't want to wait. Save room for dessert, too!

SOHO SOUTH CAFE 235 1633

Soho South Cafe
a restaurant
&
art gallery

35....RESTAURANTS

STARLAND CAFÉ
11 E. 41ST STREET
912-443-9355
MONDAY-FRIDAY 11-3

Starland Café is the place to go
for lunch if you are in Savannah
during the week and feel like ven-
turing out of "downtown" into the
midtown area known as Starland.
Starland Café is only open during
the week, but it is a great place
to get a sandwich or salad. It is
located immediately next to the
Starland Dog Park, so if you are
like me and miss your pets when
you travel, you can eat your lunch
while watching dogs frolic. They
have a Mexican salad with tortilla
chips and homemade guacamole
tossed in a spicy chipotle dressing
that is mouth-watering, and I also
really like their "CBG" sandwich
(chicken, bacon and guacamole).
After lunch, you might want to
grab a brownie, cupcake, or some
banana pudding at ***Back in the
Day Bakery*** (Page 49).

THE TEA ROOM

7 E. BROUGHTON STREET
912-239-9690
MONDAY-SATURDAY 10-5 (LUNCH IS SERVED FROM
11:30-4, AFTERNOON AND FULL TEA 2:30-4)
WWW.SAVANNAHTEAROOM.COM

Located right on Broughton Street, in the midst of
the hustle and bustle of downtown, is the most dainty
ladies' lunching spot around. While kids are welcome
and there is a small table especially for the little ones,
it has more of an elegant, adult ambience. With a huge
array of teas and a rather diverse menu, you are sure
to find something that appeals to all of the people in
your group. Sometimes, the service can be a little
slow, so this is not the place to come if you are run-
ning in for a quick bite. It is more about the experience and is well worth the wait, in my opinion. My
friend got a whiskey tea there that was served flaming.
So, for those of you who think tea is boring and stuffy,
you might want to try that one. Not to mention that
adorable gift shop in the foyer of the restaurant...

Toucan Café
531 Stephenson Avenue
912-352-2233
Monday-Thursday 11:30-2:30; 5-9
Friday-Saturday 11:30-2:30; 5-10
www.toucancafe.com

Again, I am totally going against my stick-to-downtown plan, but Toucan Café is such a cute place that even though it's about a ten-minute drive from downtown, it's worth mentioning. When I was growing up, Toucan's was a tiny little café with a handful of tables right next to the movie theater. In fact, my first date was there after seeing Teenage Mutant Ninja Turtles II. While I couldn't appreciate the genius of Toucan's at age 14, everyone else in Savannah did, and Toucan's became so popular, you couldn't get a table most nights. With delicious fresh fish dishes and some hints of the Mediterranean, Toucan Café has something for everyone and is a great spot for lunch or dinner. Thank goodness they have a much bigger restaurant these days. It's a little hidden, though, so look for the sign on Stephenson Avenue. While you are on this side of town, might as well paint some pottery at *Starlight Pottery* (Page 98), grab a cookie at *Two Smart Cookies* (Page 61), and check out the adorable clothes at *Palm Avenue* (Page 82). During the week, Toucan's can get rather crowded at lunch, so try to get there before 11:45 or after 1:00, or expect to wait a little bit.

vic's on the river

26 e. bay street
912-721-1000
sunday-saturday 11-4
sunday-thursday 4-10
friday-saturday 4-11
www.vicsontheriver.com

Vic's isn't just a ladies' only spot
like many of those previously
mentioned. It's also a great date or
group dinner venue and is fabulous for lunch or dinner! It backs
up to the river, so get a table by
the window if you can. The menu
is interesting and very Savannah – everything from shrimp and
grits to barbeque to fresh fish to
salads. The calamari appetizer and
the fried green tomato appetizer
are phenomenal. Be careful if
you wear heels in there, though,
because the floors are kind of slick.
I totally busted my butt with some
colleagues not once, but twice. I
suppose that's the price short girls
pay for trying to be fashionable
and not look up everyone's noses.
Stupid high heels.

THE WHIMSICAL TEA CUP

1710 ABERCORN STREET
912-401-0145
TUESDAY-SATURDAY 11-3

Ladies only please! This adorable slice of heaven is not even well known by many locals, but it is a MUST for all women who appreciate pink and all things girly. It is totally a hidden gem, and oddly enough, located right next to a tattoo studio, but once you see the bright pink awning, you know you have arrived. You walk in and it is all pink with chandeliers and princess decor galore! There is even a dressing area where one can adorn yourself with boas, hats, gloves and jewels (I think this is more for the younger patrons, but I dress up every time.). The menu is small– a few salads, a few sandwiches, and a quiche of the day that is always great and comes with a side salad that is delish. For the little ones, be sure to get the pink hot cocoa with pink marshmallows! And save room for dessert – their cupcakes are the icing on the (cup)cake!

zunzi's
108 e. YORK STReeT
912-443-9555
monday-saturday 11-6
www.zunzis.com

If the weather is nice, there is a hole-in-the-wall South
African restaurant that is out of this world! There is no
inside seating - just an outdoor patio, but the food is phenomenal. Often, the lunchtime rush means a line wrapped
around the building, so you want to try to get there on the
early side or after 1:00, when the lunch rush dies down. I
have never had a bad meal there, but I am convinced their
lasagna is the best ever. Also, be sure to get a glass of
their South African sweet iced tea – it's super refreshing!

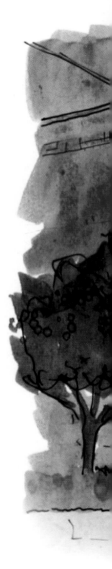

SNACKS AND DRINKS

Back in the Day Bakery

2403 BULL STREET
912-495-9292
TUESDAY-FRIDAY 9-5
SATURDAY 8-3
WWW.BACKINTHEDAYBAKERY.COM

In the up-and-coming, funky area known as Starland is this cute corner café. It has mostly sweets, but there are some delectable sandwiches and quiches, too. I would highly recommend the homemade banana pudding. They also have these adorable little mini cupcakes – perfect to just pop in your mouth and give you that little kick you need to get you through the afternoon – and fabulous brownies! My only beef with Back in the Day is that it isn't open on Sundays (the universal out-for-breakfast day), so if you want to check it out, make sure you go on a non-Sunday.

51....SNACKS AND DRINKS

THE BOHEMIAN HOTEL: ROCKS ON THE ROOF

102 W. BAY STREET
912-721-3800
WWW.BOHEMIANHOTELSAVANNAH.COM

The Bohemian Hotel just came to Savannah in late Summer, 2009. On the roof of this swanky Kessler hotel is the coolest bar in Savannah. One of my issues with Savannah is the lack of rooftop dining, but Rocks on the Roof came into Savannah and totally capitalized on that need. Whether you go for a drink or dinner or to listen to some live music, you must go to Rocks on the Roof to check out the view. There are couches and a fire pit, so year round, this is the "it" spot! Be forewarned, though, that on a Friday or Saturday night, it can be packed on the roof! If you are averse to crowds, it might be better to go for happy hour.

FORSYTH FARMER'S MARKET
FORSYTH PARK
SATURDAY 9-1

From roughly March through November, Savannah has a great farmer's market right in Forsyth Park (near the tennis courts). It is open from 9-12 on Saturday mornings (they say 1:00, but all of the good stuff is usually picked over by then, and the vendors tend to pack up early sometimes). It is almost exclusively produce, herbs, and flowers, and you can get the freshest, most wonderful local produce there. If you come during watermelon season, there is a farmer who brings homemade watermelon juice to sell, and it just might be the best $3.00 you ever spend. As someone who decided to use 3+ hours on a Sunday afternoon to try to replicate the juice, I can tell you, it is well worth the $3.00 to buy a cup. I was sore for days – juicing a watermelon is exhausting. Not to mention the fact that we are still finding watermelon seeds in various crevices in our kitchen.

55....SNACKS AND DRINKS

LEOPOLD's ice cream
212 e. BROUGHTON STReeT
912-234-4442
SUNDAY 12-10
MONDAY-THURSDAY 11-10
FRIDAY-SATURDAY 11-11
WWW.LEOPOLDSICECREAM.COM

If you are walking downtown anywhere near Broughton Street, I would recommend having your walk culminate – or at least, break– at Leopold's on the east end of Broughton Street. They have sandwiches and salads, too, but they are known for their homemade ice cream. It really is the most perfect snack/dessert on a hot Savannah day. There is something about humidity that just lends itself to cold desserts – it's almost like a magnetic pull that is beyond our control. I sometimes wonder who my hubby would choose if given the opportunity to spend the day with peanut butter chip ice cream or me. I don't think I could blame him.

LULU'S CHOCOLATE BAR

42 MARTIN LUTHER KING, JR. BOULEVARD
912-238-2012
SUNDAY 11-3; 6-12
TUESDAY-THURSDAY 6-12
(CLOSED MONDAYS DURING THE
SUMMER MONTHS ONLY)
FRIDAY-SATURDAY 5-1
WWW.LULUSCHOCOLATEBAR.NET

Need I say more? Lulu's is the perfect
place to go for after dinner drinks and dessert. In addition to an extensive wine and
martini list, they have some of the most
delicious homemade desserts in town! I
felt a little gluttonous ordering a chocolate
martini along with my Oreo cheesecake, so
I got a key lime pie martini instead. (For
some reason, that seemed less excessive.)
They also have a delicious Sunday brunch.
But if you aren't from Georgia, you must
be forewarned that you will have to drool
at the Bloody Mary bar until 12:30, since
alcohol cannot be served until then on
Sundays in our wonderful state.

mabel francis potter's cupcake emporium

6 e. state street
912-341-8014
monday-saturday 10:30-6
sunday 12-4

This is not just any old cupcake shop. This place makes at least 50 different kinds of cupcakes. They do roughly 15 flavors each day, and I personally have had the chocolate chip cookie dough cupcake, the red velvet cupcake, the banana cream cupcake, the Oreo cupcake, the chocolate brownie cheesecake cupcake, Miss Mabel's famous buttercream cupcake, the Reese's peanut butter cupcake, and the confetti vanilla cupcake (and no, not all in the same day!). I cannot decide which is my favorite.

I considered tasting all of those as research absolutely necessary in order to properly inform others about the Emporium. My office is only a few blocks away, so when I am having a bad day, I just walk my less-than-firm derriere (I gave up trying for buns of steel in exchange for cinnamon buns) down there and have myself a cupcake.

It really is amazing what a cupcake can do for morale.

TRAVELING SAVANNAH ✳ A GIRLS GUIDE.....60

TWO SMART COOKIES

6512 WHITE BLUFF ROAD
912-353-2253
MONDAY-FRIDAY 10-5
WWW.TWOSMARTCOOKIES.COM

I am pretty sure I am the (self-appointed) president of the Two Smart Cookies fan club. Two Smart Cookies is a bit of a hike from downtown (maybe 10 minutes by car), but totally worth it! Unfortunately, they are only open Monday-Friday, so if you are coming for the weekend only, you might want to reconsider your travel plans. I am not kidding. I cannot figure out what they put in their cookies, but they are the best cookies you will ever eat! They have a bunch of different kinds, but are known for their iced cutout cookies. They are basically an iced sugar cookie. Totally fat-free. Just kidding. But in fact, they do have a fat-free chocolate chewie cookie that is incredible. Not only do their iced cookies taste good, but they are works of art! They have created a niche in Savannah doing special orders for bridal showers, baby showers and birthday parties, and they decorate these cookies like they are working on canvas. I ordered some for the book club meeting that I hosted where we read <u>Memoirs of a Geisha</u>, and they did the cookies in the shape of kimonos. Beautifully decorated kimonos. I try to find any excuse to turn an event into a Two Smart Cookies worthy event. The first day of Spring might have been a stretch, but the flowers really were wonderful.

If you are downtown and don't feel like trekking to the shop and/or if it's a weekend, you might want to pop in to the adorable **Paris Market** on Broughton Street, since their Eiffel Tower cookies are none other than Two Smart Cookies! Just a little known fact that might rock your world.

SHOPPING

BLEU BELLE

205 W. BROUGHTON STREET

912-443-0011

MONDAY-SATURDAY 10-6

SUNDAY 12-5

WWW.BLEUBELLE.COM

I hope that someday I can afford to walk into a store like Bleu Belle and not even look at price tags, because everything in there is gorgeous and so stylish, and I want it all. They have the best selection of designer jeans in town and carry Nanette Lapore, BCBG, Trina Turk, Tibi, Michael Stars, Seven, etc. I did get a BCBG dress from Bleu Belle that was marked down 50%! I wear it to the office sometimes with a work-esque cardigan just because it is way too awesome to only wear for special occasions. Check out their local jewelry, too…

CHERRY & EAST

41 DRAYTON STREET
912-225-1919
FRIDAY-SATURDAY 11-7
SUNDAY 12-5
WWW.CHERRYANDEAST.COM

What a hidden gem! I recently stumbled across Cherry & East and spent nearly an hour marveling at the fabulous bedding, aprons, gifts, candles, and baby toys in this little store. They have a rather extensive online business, but just decided to have a retail shop in the fall of 2009, and I am so glad they did! Among other things, they have the most delicious candles, lip balms and soaps. I think my husband is a bit concerned with how dangerously close this precious little store is to my office. I am a huge believer in retail therapy and what it can do for one's workplace productivity.

COPPER PENNY/SHOOZ
22 W. BROUGHTON STREET
912-629-6800
MONDAY-SATURDAY 10-7
SUNDAY 12-6
WWW.SHOPCOPPERPENNY.COM

Copper Penny carries a lot of the same brands that *Bleu Belle* (page 65) does and even a few more with their extensive shoe section. Their stuff is so fun and trendy, and I sometimes find they have more in my price range than other high-end boutiques. Don't get me wrong – I have a wish list there a mile long, but I got a Michael Stars dress there for $48 and some BCBGirls shoes for $69. Not too bad! And they also have some fabulous (and rather affordable) accessories! And don't be intimidated by the size zero sales girls– they might look gorgeous in everything they try on, but there is something to be said for a little junk in the trunk, if you catch my drift.

ECLECTIBLES
10 W. BROUGHTON STREET
912-443-9292
MONDAY-SATURDAY 10:30-5
SUNDAY 10:30-3

This is a hard store to describe, but all I can say is that
every time I go in, I find something cuter and more unique
than my previous visit. It is right in the middle of Broughton Street, so there is no excuse not to stop in. They have
some artwork, lots of beachy-style crafts, great gift ideas,
and even some house wares. This is the perfect place to
find a "bring me back something from Savannah"
gift for a friend.

E. SHAVER BOOKSELLERS
326 BULL STREET
912-234-7257
MONDAY-SATURDAY 9-6

I don't know about you, but I love quaint little local bookstores. E. Shaver has been around forever, and has a charm that the big box book sellers could never replicate. It's in an old house, and it's remarkable how they managed to organize the books by genre from room to room. If you like bookstores, you should definitely check it out. There is even a special section above the mantle for local authors (i.e,....ME!).

GINGERBREAD HOUSE BRIDAL

1917 BULL STREET
912-239-9652
TUESDAY-FRIDAY 10-5:30
SATURDAY 10-3
WWW.THEGINGERBREADHOUSEBRIDAL.COM

If you are in need of anything wedding-
related, look no further than Kathy Wood and
her staff at The Gingerbread House. Not only
do they have the best selection of wedding
dresses, bridesmaid's dresses, etc. in town, but
the women who work there really know how
to make a lady feel like a princess. Seriously,
I found myself going in there on my lunch
hour during the weeks leading up to my wedding just to say hello and "check on things."
I always went back to work feeling prettier,
thinner and smarter than before I'd left. If you
want to try on dresses on a Saturday, appointments are recommended (and you will want
to make one – that way, the focus is
totally on YOU!).

James Gunn

112 W. BROUGHTON STREET
912-790-7500
MONDAY-SATURDAY 10-6
SUNDAY 12-5
www.JAMESGUNNONLINE.COM

James Gunn is similar in the brands it carries to ***Copper Penny*** (page 70) and ***Bleu Belle*** (page 65). Their stuff is funky and trendy, yet classy. They only carry the highest quality designers' clothes, but be prepared to spend a pretty penny. James Gunn carries everything from Nanette Lapore classic blouses to bohemian chic sundresses to designer jeans to drop-dead-gorgeous formalwear. You will make heads turn, though, so go on with your bad self!

La Paperie

409 Whitaker Street
912-443-9349
Monday-Saturday 10-5
www.lapaperie.net

Men totally cannot understand the appeal of paper stores. For some reason, stationery and silk ribbon and notecards and papergoods are so much fun to buy! If you are into this stuff, you must check out La Paperie. It is in a really cute little area off of Whitaker Street known as the Design District with antiques, clothing, and furniture shops. While in the Design District, you should also check out *One Fish, Two Fish, No. Four Eleven,* and *Mint.* La Paperie does beautiful work personalizing stationery and cards. Just a warning, though, I think the store smells divine, but my mom says the strong perfume smell in the shop makes her eyes water. Sometimes, we have to persevere for darling ribbons and cards, Mom.

palm avenue

5525 abercorn street
912-692-1171
monday-saturday 10-6
sunday 1-5

This is another one of my favorites that is not downtown but is for sure worth mentioning. It's a short trip by car from downtown (probably 10 minutes or less) and has some of the sweetest clothes for women and little girls (There is a small guys' section, too, but it is predominantly a ladies' place.). The majority of their clothes are Lily Pulitzer, who, in case you are unaware, is a designer with the brightest, happiest styles and colors – lots of pinks and greens. Palm Avenue's stuff is a little pricey for me, but they often have good sales, and it is really worth the trip just to look around and make a mental wish list (or splurge – you ARE on vacation, after all).

SHOP SCAD

340 BULL STREET
912-525-5180
MONDAY, TUESDAY, WEDNESDAY 9-5:30
THURSDAY & FRIDAY 9-8
SATURDAY 10-8
SUNDAY 12-5
WWW.SHOPSCADONLINE.COM

SCAD students and alumni showcase their talents and sell their wares at Shop SCAD. I have seen some of the coolest jewelry and clothing and crafts EVER in this store. It is amazing to see the talent of these current and former students. It really is a must-see!

TERRA COTTA

34 BARNARD STREET
912-236-6150
MONDAY-SATURDAY 10-6
SUNDAY 10-5

Terra Cotta is glorious – it has everything from baby clothes and gifts to Hobo handbags to shoes to one-of-a-kind Anthropologie-esque clothes. Their stuff is high end but very worth it, and you can usually find some good deals on the sale rack. I got some of my girlfriends plush robes from there last year, and they swear they are the softest things they have ever put on their bodies. While you are there, you should definitely pop in next door to **Kitchens on the Square** for some great kitchen basics or unique knick-knacks. My bestie, Beth, got an Elvis cutting board for her mom there. Whose kitchen isn't complete without an Elvis cutting board?

ACTIVITIES

BEADSTRO

226 W. BROUGHTON STREET
912-232-2334
MONDAY-FRIDAY 11-6
SATURDAY-SUNDAY 12-5
(THEY STOP MAKING JEWELRY ONE
HOUR PRIOR TO CLOSING)
WWW.BEADSTRO.COM

Lisa and Danielle and the rest of the Beadstro staff are fabulous. You can go in and pick out beads and they will either teach you to make the jewelry yourself or string it for you while you wait. For those of you who have never beaded before, do not be intimidated. And do not think it is an entire afternoon commitment. I took three little girls (ages 6, 7, and 9) on a Sunday afternoon, and we were in and out (beautifully adorned in hand-made jewels, no less) in about an hour and a half. What a cool way to have a beautiful reminder of your Savannah trip and pick up a new hobby and skill. I am a beader myself, but I will find pictures of more complicated pieces in magazines and bring them to Beadstro, and the staff will teach me how to make it exactly like in the picture. It really gets your creative juices flowing and is so much fun. I have been making jewelry as my relaxation craft of choice for a long time. You can check out my stuff at www.beadsbymer.com if you feel so inclined (please forgive my shameless plug).

CHEF JOE RANDALL'S COOKING SCHOOL
5409 WATERS AVENUE
912-303-0409
WEDNESDAY-SATURDAY 6:30-9:30
WWW.CHEFJOERANDALL.COM

When a friend at work asked me to take a cooking class with her for $60, I thought she was nuts. But, my hubby and I went, and I am so glad we did. This is not just any cooking class – you sit around a large counter, and basically Chef Joe prepares the most delicious meal for you, explaining what he is doing every step of the way. His wife serves the patrons wine, and the food is better than you could find in most restaurants. There are multiple courses, and each night, there is a different theme/menu. To top it off, you get copies of the recipes, so that when the wine wears off, you actually remember what went into your delicious meal. Reservations are required.

savannaH movie Tours

301 Martin LuTHer King, JR. Boulevard
912-234-3440
Daily at 3 OR 4
www.savannaHmovieTours.com

Having grown up in Savannah, I am
not one to recommend a tour, but I
took this one and loved it! I promise
you will be shocked at how many
movies were filmed in Savannah – *Midnight in the Garden of
Good and Evil, The Legend of
Bagger Vance, Forces of Nature*
(I never said they were good
movies), *Glory, Forrest Gump,
The General's Daughter, Something to Talk About,* just to name
a few…. The tour is set up so
that you are on a small bus and
clips of movies are shown on
the screens overhead. Right
after a clip is shown, you will
pass the exact spot where the
clip was filmed! It is really a
non-cheesy way to see a lot
of downtown and is really a
good time. The tour I took
was 90 minutes long and
cost $25 per person ($15
for kids), but apparently,

there is a "VIP Movie Tour" where you see everything I saw but you also stop
at various places along the way to eat and drink. It's a bit more costly - $195
for adults and $185 for kids. You must have 4 or more people to reserve spots
and must reserve your spots 14 days in advance, and the tour lasts 4.5 hours! I
really want to go. I mean, it is very important research…

savannah theatre

222 BULL STREET
912-233-7764
www.savannahtheatre.com

Who doesn't love a night at the theater? While it might not be Broadway, it's still fabulous! The theater is gorgeous, and since it's rather small, all of the seats are VIP. Some great shows rotate through here, and shows are usually at 8:00 on Tuesday- Saturday nights with 3:00 matinees on Saturday and Sunday. The prices are certainly better than Broadway - $35.00 for adults and $16.00 for anyone under 17. Don't run off right after the show, because all of the performers come out into the lobby right afterwards to sign autographs and schmooze. That, my friends, makes it cooler than Broadway!

And if you are so inspired by the show that you want to go sing yourself, right across from the Theater is **McDonough's**, the city's best karaoke bar! What have you got to lose – you are visiting, so most people won't even know you. I tend to use another name when I sign up to sing, anyway. I prefer not to think of it as lying but rather as my alter-ego. Jessie Spano is a favorite of mine. I was using Steve Sanders for awhile (not because I liked him on 90210 but because I feel he got an unfairly bad reputation and was often mistreated by the female characters while having to sport that awful blond, curly mullet), but I tended to get funny looks; apparently, I don't look like a Steve. My caveat to you about **McDonough's,** though, is that it is so popular that the line to sing can be rather long. One night, after a rather festive holiday party, I was really feeling the need to show Savannah what I could do and went to **McDonough's** but was told there were 30 songs ahead of me in line to sing! Total buzz kill.

The other negative about **McDonough's** is that it
can be rather smoky inside. There is nothing worse than having
to dry clean your super cute outfit and wash your hair AGAIN after you leave a
smoky bar. I guess it's a price we pay to sing some good karaoke, my friends.

STARLIGHT POTTERY
7070 HODGSEN MEMORIAL DRIVE
912-303-9599
WWW.STARLIGHTPOTTERY.COM

Another activity that gets your creative juices flowing is pottery painting. While sadly the shop in Savannah is no longer located downtown, it is worth the trek (10 minutes by car from downtown). The studio is in a strip center, so keep your eyes peeled. If you have never painted pottery before, you must try it. You get to pick out an undecorated, boring piece of pottery and paint it until it is a work of art. They have a huge selection of pottery you can paint, and you glaze and decorate it to your heart's content and then leave it for them to fire for you. Depending on the length of your trip, you can arrange to come back and pick it up, or the staff will send it to you. This is one of the perfect things to do on a ridiculously hot or rainy Savannah day. Oh, and make sure you bring a bottle of wine and some snacks along– they don't sell any food or drink there, but you are welcome to bring some with you. It might be rather enlightening to see what you come up with after a glass or two of wine…

SPAS AND PAMPERING

GLOW (located in Bungalow)

204 W. Broughton Street
912-944-2550
Monday-Saturday 10-6
Sunday 12-5
www.glowsavannah.com

I have a feeling I am not the only one who hopes to return from a vacation with a tan. I also know that sometimes the weather gods do not help us with our tanning goals, and sometimes, our trips draw to a close with our skin not quite as bronze as we would like. This is where Glow comes in! Glow is conveniently located on Broughton Street in the heart of your shopping excursions and is tucked inside this adorable boutique. While they do waxing and threading and facials, too, if you appreciate a sun-kissed hue like I do (without the UV harm – my dermatologist would be so proud), you should check out Glow's spray tans. A tan is only $35.00 and will last about a week – long enough for you to get the jealous looks from colleagues for a full work week when you return from vacation. I would recommend, though that you not get spray tanned for the first time prior to a major event, just because you never know how your skin might react. You also might not want to go trying on clothes right afterwards, since you might leave your mark, if you know what I mean.

magnolia spa (at the marriott riverfront)

100 general mcintosh boulevard
912-373-2039
sunday-monday 9-6
tuesday-saturday 9-7

I have tried various spas in town for services (necessary research, of course), and I must admit that I was surprised to find that I enjoyed the service and consistency of the spa at the Marriott the most. I can attest to the facial and massage and waxing services there and all were wonderful. They recently began offering hard wax, which, for those of you who do not know, is a Godsend. It is a teal (or sometimes purple or gold – just think Mardi-Gras colors) wax that grips onto the hair itself (rather than to your skin) and then hardens into a strip (no paper required) that is then pulled off. There is much less irritation and redness (and pain) than is typical with old-fashioned wax. In fact, for me, the redness is usually gone within 30 minutes (as opposed to hours with regular wax). So, if you didn't have time to get "cleaned up" before leaving for your vacation (or maybe the man you are with could use some man-scaping?) and don't want to be that girl with the red forehead and lip that often comes with waxing, consider your problem solved!

Salon Della Vita

128 W. LIBERTY STREET
912-231-0427
TUESDAY-SATURDAY 9-4 (WILL STAY
OPEN LATER IF APPOINTMENTS)
www.salondellavita.com

Not a lot of salons will take walk-ins
or last-minute appointments, but Salon
Della Vita will, and they do a fabulous
job! For those of you who have never
come to Savannah and didn't know about
the intense humidity, you might be say-
ing to your hair: "Why won't you stay
smooth? Why are you flying in every
direction? You don't usually look like
this." This is the time, friend, when you
need to make a quick appointment at (or
just pop in to!) Salon Della Vita to have
your hair washed and styled. I'm not sure
what it is about a trained stylist doing
your hair that makes it look so much
better than when we do it ourselves, but
it's a proven fact that it does. Prices for
washing and styling vary depending on
the length of your hair, but trust me when
I say that they are the most affordable of
the high-end salons I have tried in town.

see jane

323 W. BROUGHTON STREET
912-234-1080
MONDAY-SATURDAY 10-7
SUNDAYS BY APPOINTMENT ONLY
WWW.SEEJANESHOP.COM

See Jane is not just your typical nail salon; it is a fun and funky approach to beautifying! They call it "a modern apothecary and beauty bar," but to the lay people (like me), it is a friendly, trendy top-notch manicure/pedicure, facial and make-up place. If you are about to hit a night on the town, you should definitely go get your make-up done! It's only $20.00, and while they do take walk-ins, it might be a good idea to make an appointment, because they can fill up. They have ladies' nights on Thursdays where you get a complimentary cocktail with your service. Having a cocktail while getting my nails done with my girlfriends? Um…yes please! The employees are just wonderful, and I could spend days smelling all of the bubble baths, lotions, and scrubs! Oooohh la la…

Since you are already on the West end of Broughton Street, you should go to the next corner, take a right, and check out *Red Clover.* I must admit that I recently discovered this gem of a boutique and am so glad that I did. The clothes, jewelry, and shoes were just the right mix of classic and trendy, and the prices were ultra reasonable. I got two (if my husband asks, it was buy one, get one free) blouses, each so unique with just a touch of embroidery (I have a weakness for embroidery.) for $64 total. No buyer's remorse there, my friends.

sweetwater day spa (aka terme acqua dolce)

148 abercorn street
912-233-3288
monday-saturday 10-6
sunday 12-6
www.termeacquadolce.com

Now, you have to look carefully, because Sweetwater is not the most well-marked spa in town. I am pretty sure I have tried every spa here in Savannah, being the facial and massage lover that I am (again, I justified this as being necessary research in order to accurately inform Savannah visitors of the best). While I loved my massage and facial at Sweetwater, I must say their pedicure was the best I have ever had. First of all, I walked in and was offered this delicious fruity champagne cocktail. Then, I sat in this uber comfortable chair that you had to step up to so that it was like a throne and your feet were at eye level with the pedicurist. Go, my friends, and be a princess - a princess with well-manicured feet! They are open on Saturdays and Sundays, which is a rarity and awesome for weekend visitors!

WHERE TO MEET MEN

I have to put in a major disclaimer here (being the lawyer that I am) and warn you that this is not my area of expertise these days. Having found my Prince Charming, I am rather removed from the dating scene. What I do know is that **Saya, Cha Bella, Il Pasticcio, Molly MacPherson's Scottish Pub, Circa 1875, Jazz'd** (Page 29), and **Rocks on the Roof** (Page 52) are all rather trendy hot spots. If you prefer a more casual courting scene, I would recommend checking out **Wild Wings** or **Loco's**. Both often have live music on the weekend nights. I will warn you, though, if you are not into the dirty white baseball cap/fraternity t-shirt kind of guy, you might want to avoid **Wild Wings** and **Loco's**. If gentlemen of the military variety tend to tickle your fancy, **Wild Wings** might also be a good option for you. You can also find a handful of good soldiers right down from **Wild Wings** at **Bar Bar**. Be wary of the stairs leading to **Bar Bar**, though, after a few drinks. Most men are not so drawn to a woman cascading down a set of stairs. If the artsy variety tickles your fancy, you should check out **Pinkie Masters, The American Legion,** or **Hangfire**. Best of luck, ladies, in your search for Mr. Right. I found mine in Savannah, so maybe you will too…

WHEN TO COME TO SAVANNAH

FIRST SATURDAYS (OF EACH MONTH, MARCH-DECEMBER)

While Savannah is wonderful any time of year (give or take some heat and gnats), there are certain times that Savannah has even more to offer. With the exception of January and February, the first weekend of every month has loads happening down on River Street. On the Friday night before the first Saturday of the month, there are fireworks down by the river, and then, on that Saturday, there are street vendors selling tons of cool local crafts all along the riverfront. There are food vendors and usually some form of music, too. The biggest First Saturday month by far is October. The first weekend in October is known as Oktoberfest, and it is the typical first Saturday festivities and then some. The highlight for me, as a dog lover, is the ever-famous Wiener Dog Races. Yes, you read that correctly. The races have become so popular that people from all over come with their dachshunds to see who has the fastest little legs in Savannah.

ST. PATRICK'S DAY

For those of you who have not heard of Savannah's huge St. Patrick's Day festivities, you might want to get out more, because that is a pretty good indication that you are clueless. No offense, but it's kind of a big deal. Savannah has one of the biggest St. Patrick's Day celebrations in the Country (second only to New York!). Savannah becomes party central – a la New Orleans during Mardi Gras or Tampa during Gasparilla – during the week of St. Patrick's Day. Maybe it's because I grew up going downtown and experiencing the parade every year or maybe it's because I am a gigantic dork, but I, personally, would not recommend coming to Savannah during this time if you truly want to experience the glory and beauty of Savannah. The town is always beautiful, but during St. Pat's, downtown is packed to the brim with non-Savannahians and some of Savannah's beauty might be hidden by beer bottles, beads, and boobies.
But if that's your thing, have at it!

savannah music festival

www.savannahmusicfestival.com

If you are a music person at all, you should try to plan your trip in March/April so that it overlaps with some of the world-renowned Savannah Music Festival. The festival lasts for roughly a month, and there are multiple acts of all kinds all over the city every night. People come from all over for a night or two or even longer to see the acts. It really is awesome and so unique to Savannah. During that month, the evenings are extra lively around downtown with everyone going in and out of performances. Check out the schedule at the website to see if any acts tickle your fancy. Last year, my hubby and I saw Doyle Lawson (total bluegrass God) and the Lovell Sisters, and this year, we are seeing Cherry Holmes and one of my most talented friends, Kristina Train. She and I went to high school together here in Savannah, and I kind of feel famous knowing her because she's a pretty big deal and super fabulous!

savannah jazz festival

www.savannahjazzfestival.org

During the last full week of September every year, various downtown venues host the famous Jazz Festival. I'm not going to lie – I used to think that all jazz music belonged in an elevator or an old folks home, but having married into a family of musicians, I am beginning to appreciate how beautiful a well-played saxophone can be. There are some pretty big names (that go right over my head, but impress the heck out of my husband, dad, and father-in-law) that come to Savannah to play in the festival. If you are a jazz fan, you should definitely check out the schedule, because best of all, the shows are FREE!

SAVANNAH GREEK FESTIVAL

Every year, for a week in October at St. Paul's Greek Orthodox Church, the Greek community hosts the Greek Festival. There are music, dancing, crafts, and some of the best Greek food you will ever eat. I didn't realize how awesome it was until I actually went to Greece on my honeymoon and discovered that the food at Savannah's Greek Festival is even better. The people are always super friendly, and it really is a great time.

JEWISH FOOD FESTIVAL

I suppose I am a bit biased being Jewish and all, but I happen to LOVE the Jewish Food Festival, aka "Shalom Y'all." Always held in conveniently located Forsyth Park on the last Sunday in October, Shalom Y'all consists of various booths selling everything from bagels and lox to noodle kugel (not as good as yours, Mom) to Rabbi Belzer's famous Amen Lo-mein. There is music and usually a really fun crowd. The festival starts mid-morning and goes until 3:00, but every year, some of the booths start to run out of food by 1:30. I know this from experience as a 2009 Shalon Y'all Blintz Station volunteer.

TOUR OF HOMES AND GARDENS
WWW.SAVANNAHTOUROFHOMES.ORG

Some women (i.e., my mom and my bff, Beth) like to take tours of the most beautiful homes and gardens downtown Savannah has to offer. When they drag me with them, I will admit the places are exquisite, but I find the whole event kind of a tease and slightly unfair. I mean, sure, your 6,000 square foot estate in immaculate condition and with closets bigger than my bedroom is nice, but why doesn't anyone want to tour my 1,100 square foot cottage? I can't help but feel that the tour of homes is a bit prejudiced against the little guy. If you are like my mom and Beth, though, and like to learn about the history and architecture of some of the city's finest homes and properties, you should look into the tour. It takes place at the end of March each year over the course of a weekend and then again around the holidays. Check it out (but heed my warning)....

savannaH college of art and Design Fashion SHOW
www.scaD.eDu

If you are even remotely into fashion, you might
want to consider looking into strutting your stuff
at the SCAD annual fashion show. Held each
year in May (dates vary, so check the website
for specifics and ticket info), the show features
the work of the best of SCAD's fashion program
and is attended by some tres famous fashion and
style people (who I probably wouldn't recognize
if I fell on them, but that really means nothing
with respect to their importance). However, there
is usually a big name celebrity designer (one year
it was Vera Wang and another, Marc Jacobs) and
celebrities are often in attendance (i.e., Michael
Douglas and Catherine Zeta-Jones). I'm warning you, though; you are about to hob-nob with
the trendiest of the trendy, so you might want
to think long and hard about your attire. If you
wear anything even slightly resembling a fanny
pack or acid washed high-waist jeans (a la A.C.
Slater in Saved by the Bell, but no offense to
Mario Lopez, since he wore them quite well circa
1990…and I know they're coming back, but I'm
still vehemently opposed to them), I'll deny any
connection to you.

savannaH Film Festival
www.scaD.eDu/FilmFest

Another fun festival hosted by SCAD each year is the Film Festival. Featuring
both well-known filmmakers and rising stars, the festival lasts for a week during the end of October and early November. With multiple shows each night
all over downtown, you'll have plenty of opportunities to see some great

movies at Savannah's finest theaters. This event has totally become a place to see and be seen. So, again, dress cute or we will no longer be friends. Check out the schedule of shows at the SCAD-tastic (a word invented by yours truly that basically means funky, trendy, and way cooler than anything I could have come up with) website.

GETTING AROUND SAVANNAH

Savannah is totally a walking City, but my husband and I decided to rent one of those little mini cars to tour around for a day, and it was so much fun! It's like a convertible but better because you don't have to fill it with gas and it fits in the tiniest of parking spaces! They can fit 2, 4, or 6 people. Check them out at www. savannahcruisers.com. For the slightly more adventuresome is the Vespa rental: www.vespasavannah.com. I am going to be honest – Vespas kind of scare me, but once I saw the fun colors and the fact that some have flowers painted on them, I calmed down a bit. I mean, florals can't possibly be dangerous (except when paired with plaids or paisley prints). The cool thing about Vespas is that it is legal to park them on the sidewalks in Savannah, so no hunting for parking spots and more time to shop and play!

FOR THE ATHLETIC WOMAN

If exercising is part of your weekend regimen (props to you, by the way), you should look into renting a bike for your stay in Savannah. Savannah is such a cool town to bike in, since some of the niche areas can be blocks apart and can take a little while to walk between. Check out www.sekkabicycles.com for bike rentals right on Broughton Street. There are some great bike trails out towards Tybee Island starting at Fort Pulaski. You will also definitely want to make your way to Forsyth Park for a walk or run. Not only is it a beautiful park and a great place to people watch but it is also the ideal exercise track – 1.5 miles around, partially shaded and lots going on! You might also like to venture out to Tybee Island for a kayak excursion. *Sea Kayak Georgia* has rentals and optional guided trips: www.seakayakgeorgia.com. If you do go out to Tybee, you should definitely eat at *AJ's Dockside.* They don't take reservations, and there can be a long wait, but the view at sunset is unreal: www.ajsdocksidetybee.com.

WHAT TO PACK

This is a hard one. I pretty much overdress for everything, so this is a tricky subject for me. I tend to think sundresses (and an optional cardigan) are the safest thing to wear in Savannah between March and October. That being said, there are some cooler days where pants are better (after all, how annoying is it to shave and then get goose bumps and be prickly all over again?), and in the wintertime, we can have some cold days that can feel even colder with the breeze off the Savannah River. If visiting Savannah between October and March, dressing in layers is the way to go because the high and low in a given day can span 30 degrees. My primary sartorial advice to you would be to be very careful with your shoe packing. I am 5'1", and I totally feel the need to increase my height by wearing high heels whenever possible. However, many of the squares in Savannah are brick, and not an evenly laid brick – a brick that is just right for getting your heal stuck and rolling your ankle. And River Street is the worst! River Street is made of cobblestones, so walking with heels down there is treacherous, to say the least. This is one city where I would say comfortable shoes are the way to go. Many designers are making cute flats, boots and flops these days, so I don't think it's necessary to sacrifice fashion for comfort.

SAMPLE DAYS

SATURDAY SAMPLE DAY

Assuming it's not a First Saturday, because if it is, you definitely should make your way to River Street at some point:

1. Get dressed, beautify, and twirl once in hotel mirror.
2. Head to ***Harris Baking Company*** (Page 28) for some breakfast.
3. Pop in next door to ***Motorini*** (Page 121) to rent a Vespa for the day to cruise around town.
4. Ride over to ***Sweetwater Day Spa*** (Page 109) for some pedicures.
5. Cruise around town a bit while paws are drying.
6. Make your way up Whitaker toward Broughton, stopping at ***Mint, One Fish Two Fish, La Paperie*** (Page 79) and ***No. Four Eleven*** in the Design District.
7. Dine for lunch at the ***Tea Room*** (Page 37).
8. Shop on Broughton Street, hitting ***Bleu Belle*** (Page 65), ***Copper Penny*** (Page 70), ***Terra Cotta*** (Page 86), ***James Gunn*** (Page 78), ***Cherry & East*** (Page 67) and ***Eclectibles*** (Page71).
9. Grab some ice cream at ***Leopold's*** (Page 56).
10. Back to the hotel for fashion show with new purchases and to get dressed for the evening.
11. Dinner at ***Vic's on the River*** (Page 41).
12. After-dinner drinks and dessert at ***Lulu's Chocolate Bar*** (Page 57).
13. Finish the evening with some late night karaoke at ***Mc Donough's.***

SUNDAY SAMPLE DAY

1. Put on new purchases from yesterday's shopping.
2. Head to Liberty Street for brunch at ***Soho South Cafe*** (Page 33).
3. Walk up Bull Street, stopping at ***Shop SCAD*** (Page 83), ***E. Shaver Booksellers*** (Page 74), ***Savannah Art Works,*** and ***Gallery Espresso*** (Page 23).
4. Grab a cupcake at the ***Cupcake Emporium*** (Page 60).
5. Take the afternoon ***Movie Tour*** (Page 93).
6. Pop in to ***See Jane*** (Page 108) for a professional make-up application to get you ready for your evening.
7. Stroll on over for Happy Hour at the ***Olde Pink House*** (Page 32).
8. Enjoy dinner and music at ***Jazz'd*** (Page 29).

BOOKS TO READ TO GET PSYCHED FOR YOUR SAVANNAH TRIP

<u>Savannah Blues</u> and <u>Savannah Breeze</u>
Mary Kay Andrews is awesome. These are two of my favorite books – so fun to read and both heavily centered around Savannah. While they are different, both books involve the same protagonist and her best friend. Technically, <u>Breeze</u> is the sequel to <u>Blues</u>, but I read them in the wrong order and was still able to enjoy them and not lose too much sleep in light of the mistake. The writing is super entertaining, and I'm sure you'll love the discussion of antiques and old Savannah buildings. I know I did! Both books made me want to grab a girlfriend and do something wild!

<u>Midnight in the Garden of Good and Evil</u>
Duh. I mean, this is kind of a given, but it's a book that's very Savannah. In case you're unaware (and this probably makes you the same person who didn't know that Savannah had a big St. Patrick's Day scene), <u>Midnight</u> is a book (and movie, but the book is way better) about a murder scandal in Savannah that took place in the 1980s. It was written by John Berendt and showcases some really interesting Savannah characters and scenery. The famous Lady Chablis from <u>Midnight</u> still makes occasional appearances at *Club One* downtown.

<u>Savannah from Savannah</u>
By Denise Hildreth, <u>Savannah from Savannah</u> is an entertaining story about a writer (can you guess her name?) who moves back home to Savannah when she finds out that her diva mom has been behind her literary success. She moves back home to start over as a journalist, and while slow in parts, the book is quite entertaining and provides some insight into Savannah society. There are two sequels to this one: <u>Savannah Undone</u> and <u>Savannah at the Beach</u>, but I honestly haven't read them yet. Don't judge. They are on my to-be-read list.

OUTRO

I hope I have given you some ideas as to where to go and what to do while you are in Savannah. Hopefully, you will fall in love with the city (like I have) and come back for many more visits! There are always new things to see and do, and this book only touches on all that Savannah has to offer.

THANK YOU

Thank you to my husband, Andy, for being so supportive in all of my endeavors. Not only do you embrace my quirkiness but you allow me to drag you to all of these places (except for The Whimsical Tea Cup), and you come along with a smile. I love you so much. Thank you to our dogs, Shelby, Anna, Wesley and Lewis, for always being excited to see me when I walk in the door even if I've only been gone for five minutes. I love that you are always right under my feet even despite your problem with flatulence (Anna...) and the chaos that ensues whenever there is a doorbell on TV. Thank you to my friends and family for being my editors. You know who you are. And a special thank you to my friend, Sarah Powell, for giving me the idea of writing this book! You put the fire under my butt and made me realize that I could really do it. And last but not least, thank you to my fabulous illustrator who made this book what it is. I feel lucky to have found you before you got too important to work with a non-professional writer on her first book, and I fully expect to see you soar, because your work is unique and beautiful. Thank you for taking a chance on this project.

ABOUT THE ILLUSTRATOR

Erin Salzer Hanna has been an artist and designer throughout life and many disciplines — from video to graphic design to printmaking to landscape architecture to… the list goes on. Erin grew up in New Orleans and Beaufort, SC before migrating to the north for education and experience. She holds a BFA from Carnegie Mellon University in Electronic and Time-Based Media, and a Masters of Landscape Architecture from the University of Pennsylvania. The cold temperatures of the north and a desire to be closer to family and friends brought her back south in 2004.

She currently practices in the fields of landscape architecture with her firm Erin P. Salzer Landscape Design, and graphic design as co-founder of Republic Creative Group. Erin moonlights as a Savannah Derby Devil, and enjoys crafting, antiquing, cooking, and entertaining. She lives in Savannah in a pink house with husband Jesse and German Shepherd, Duke.

xoxo,

TRAVEL NOTES

TRAVEL NOTES

TRAVEL NOTES

TRAVEL NOTES

TRAVEL NOTES

TRAVEL NOTES

TRAVEL NOTES